WITH CD

PRIMER LEVEL
GOLD STAR P ...

D0589221

PIANO

Adventures®

Challenging pieces with
changing moods and
changing hand positions

by *Nancy and Randall Faber*

A BASIC PIANO METHOD

Production: Frank J. Hackinson
Production Coordinator: Philip Groeber
Editor: Edwin McLean
Cover: Terpstra Design, San Francisco
Engraving: Tempo Music Press, Inc.
Printer: Tempo Music Press, Inc.

THE
F·J·H
MUSIC
COMPANY
INC.
Frank J. Hackinson

ISBN 1-56939-511-X

Table of Contents

("Gold Star" characteristics of each piece)

Color the star gold or put a star sticker for each piece you learn!

FF160

I Found a Penny

Words by Crystal Bowman
Music by Nancy Faber

Happy-Go-Lucky

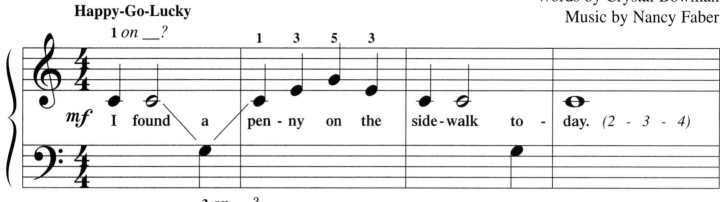

I found a pen-ny on the side-walk to-day. *(2 - 3 - 4)*

5

I put it in my pock-et where it will stay. *(2 - 3 - 4)*

Teacher Duet: (Student plays 1 octave higher)

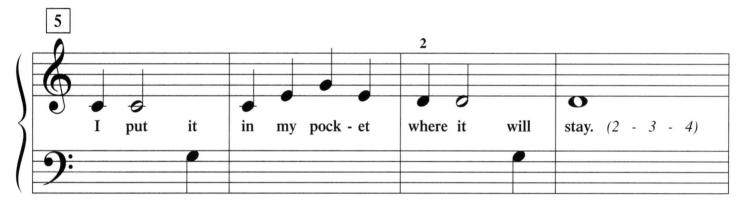

FF1602

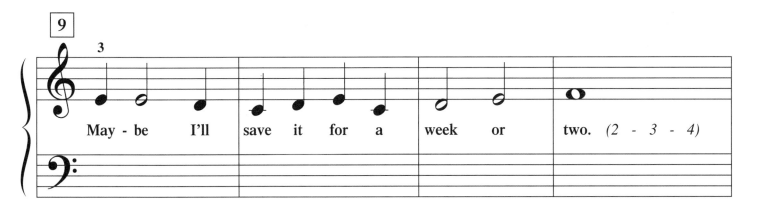

9

May - be I'll save it for a week or two. *(2 - 3 - 4)*

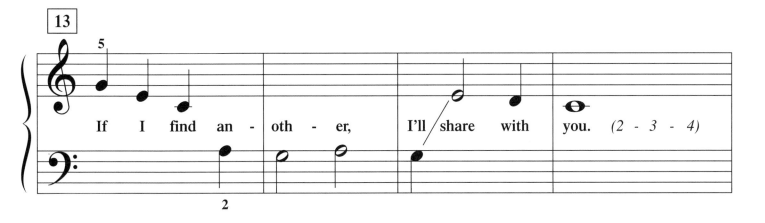

13

If I find an - oth - er, I'll share with you. *(2 - 3 - 4)*

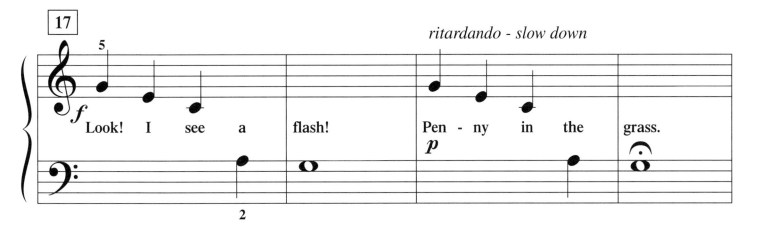

17

ritardando - slow down

f Look! I see a flash! Pen - ny in the grass.

p

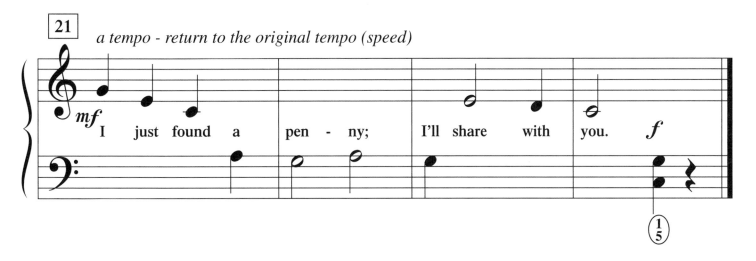

21

a tempo - return to the original tempo (speed)

mf I just found a pen - ny; I'll share with you. *f*

DISCOVERY Where are *measures 13-16* repeated later in the piece? What is new at the very end? Tell your teacher.

Pterodactyls, Really Neat

Play BOTH HANDS 2 octaves
LOWER than written.

Words by Jennifer MacLean
Music by Nancy Faber

Stomping heavily

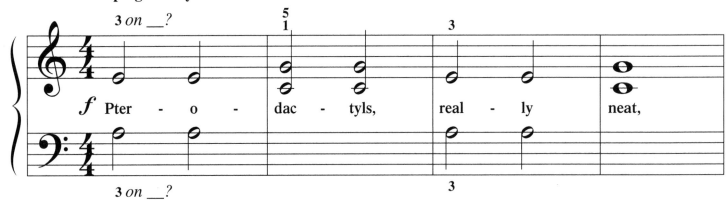

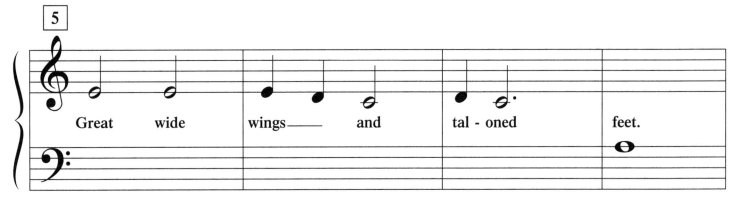

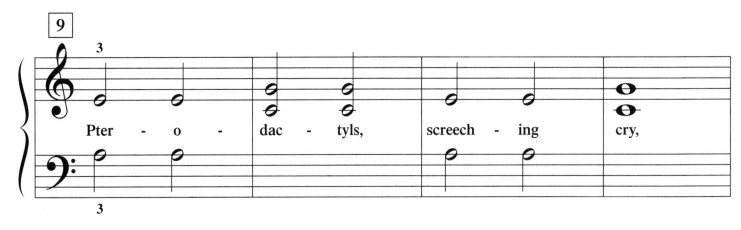

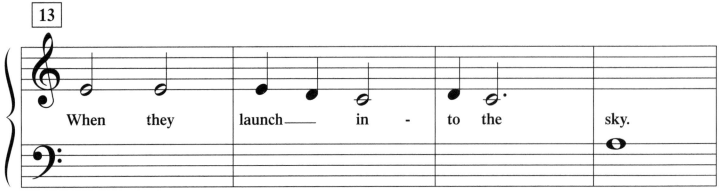

FF1602

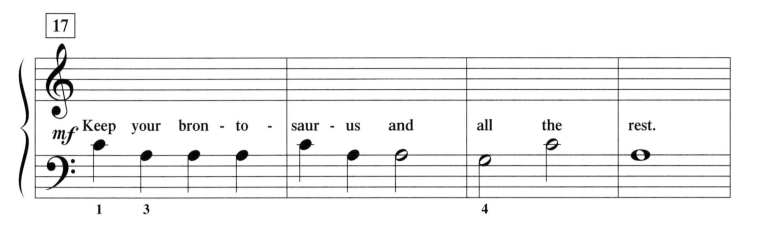

17 | mf Keep your bron - to - saur - us and all the rest.

21 | Pter - o - dac - tyls real - ly are the best. But you

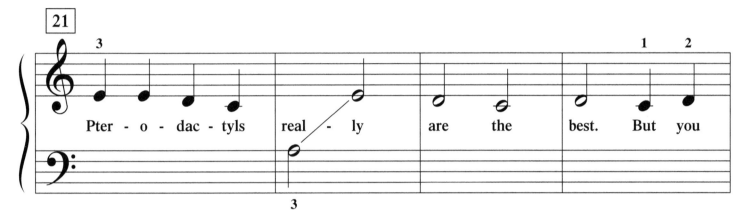

25 | f don't want one to be a guest

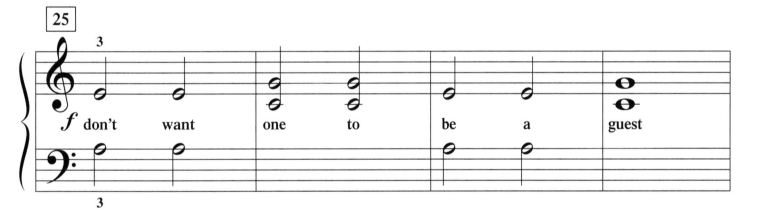

29 | on your Mon - day morn - ing spell -ing test!

ritardando

R.H. over ③

Play the 𝅗𝅥
lowest 8*va*⌐
A on the piano.

DISCOVERY Where does the *first* line of music return later in the piece? Tell your teacher.
Hint: It returns two times.

CD Instr. **Piano**

Zoom, Zoom, Witch's Broom

**Hold the damper pedal
down throughout the piece.**

Words by Jennifer MacLean
Music by Nancy Faber

Zipping along

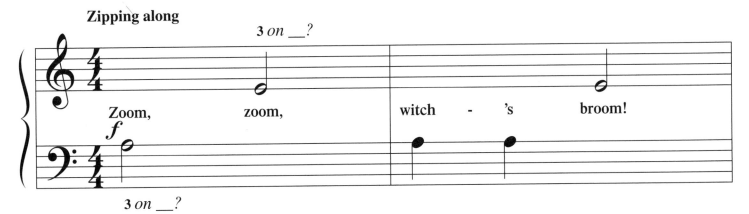

Zoom, zoom, witch - 's broom!

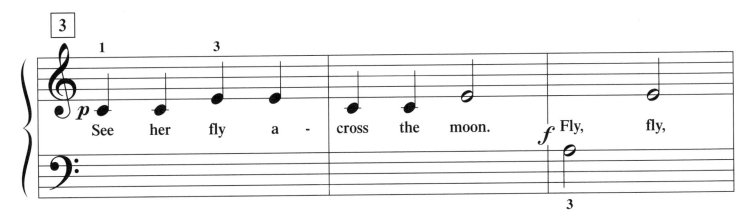

See her fly a - cross the moon. Fly, fly,

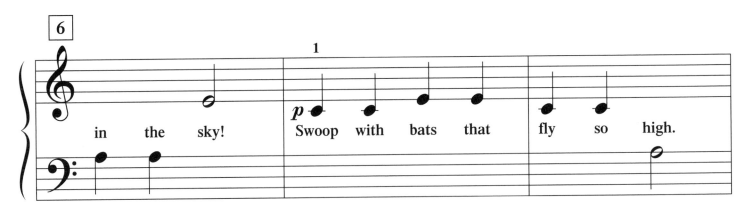

in the sky! Swoop with bats that fly so high.

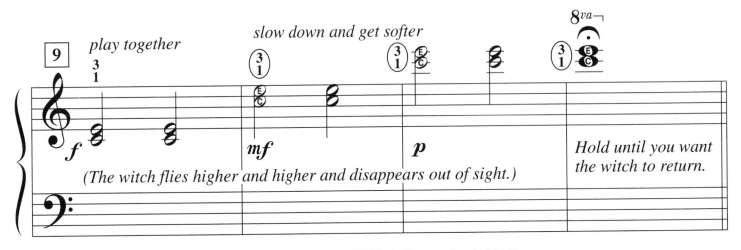

play together *slow down and get softer*

(*The witch flies higher and higher and disappears out of sight.*)

*Hold until you want
the witch to return.*

FF1602

DISCOVERY This piece uses **3 letter names** from the musical alphabet. Can you name them?

③ *Play the lowest A on the piano.*

Teacher Duet: (Student plays as written, without pedal)

CD Instr. Piano
7 8

Theme and Variations

Words and Music
by Nancy Faber

Briskly
Theme

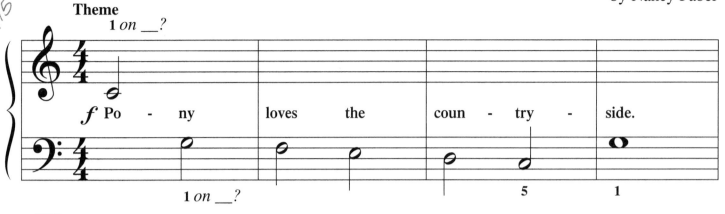

1 on __?

f Po - ny   loves   the   coun - try - side.

1 on __?

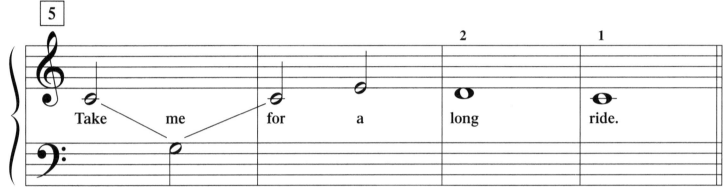

Take   me   for   a   long   ride.

Teacher Duet: (Student plays 1 octave higher)

1 **Theme**

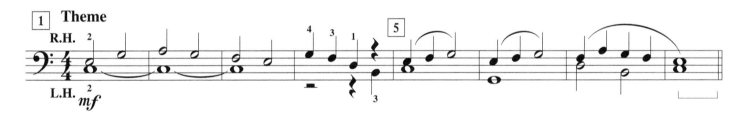

R.H.
L.H. **mf**

9 **Variation 1**

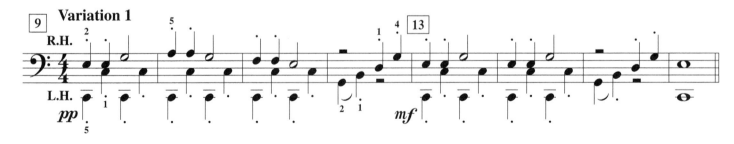

R.H.
L.H. **pp**   **mf**

17 **Variation 2**

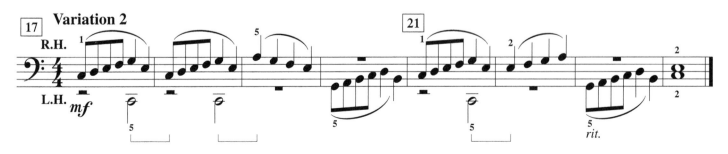

R.H.
L.H. **mf**   *rit.*

FF1602

9 Variation 1

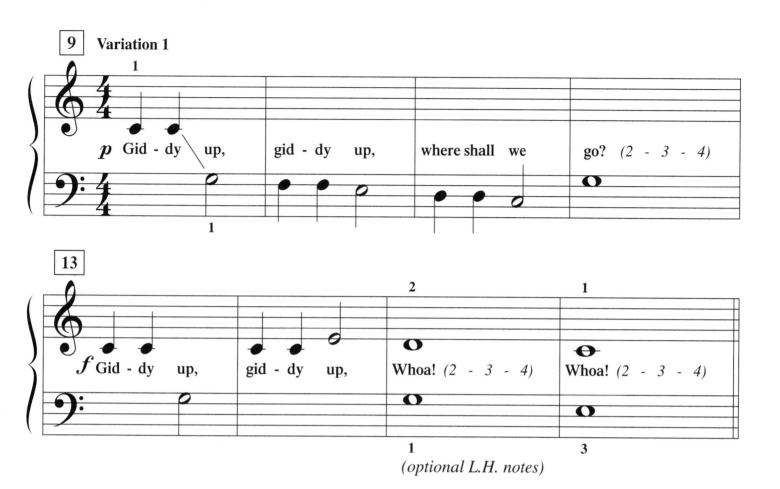

p Gid - dy up, gid - dy up, where shall we go? *(2 - 3 - 4)*

13

f Gid - dy up, gid - dy up, Whoa! *(2 - 3 - 4)* Whoa! *(2 - 3 - 4)*

(optional L.H. notes)

17 Variation 2

keep the beat

f Po - ny, po - ny, gal - lop ver - y fast.

21

Po - ny, take me to the barn at last!
ritardando

DISCOVERY

Which **variation** is your favorite? Tell your teacher why.

CD Instr. **Piano**
9 **10**

A Rainbow Is a Smile
(Turned Upside Down)

Words by Crystal Bowman
Music by Nancy Faber

Gently, smooth and connected

mf E - ven though it's rain - ing, I'll not frown, for a

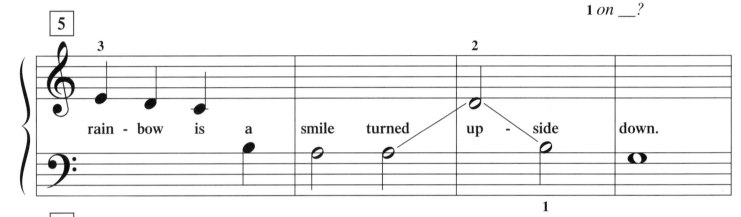

rain - bow is a smile turned up - side down.

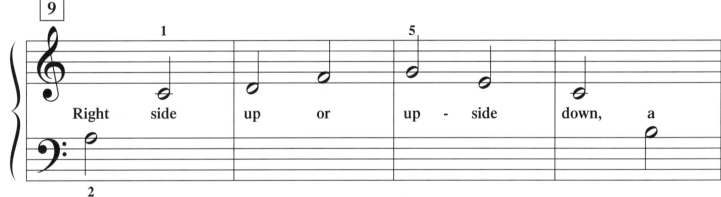

Right side up or up - side down, a

Teacher Duet: (Student plays 1 octave higher, without pedal)

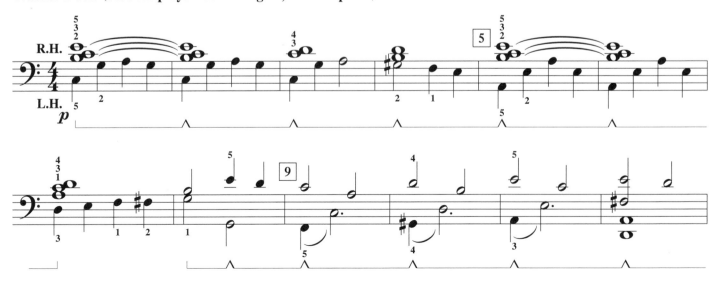

FF1602

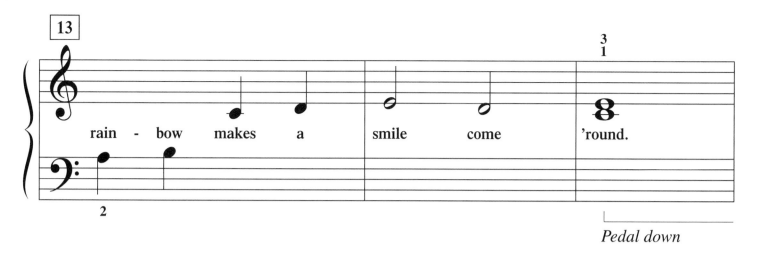

Pedal down

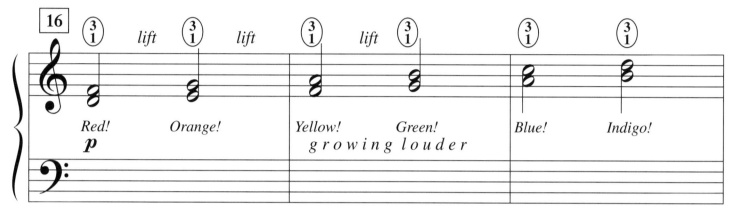

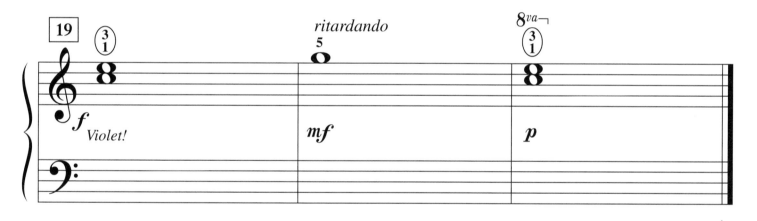

Lift pedal.

DISCOVERY Hold the pedal down and play 3rds *high* on the piano. Listen to the ringing sounds!

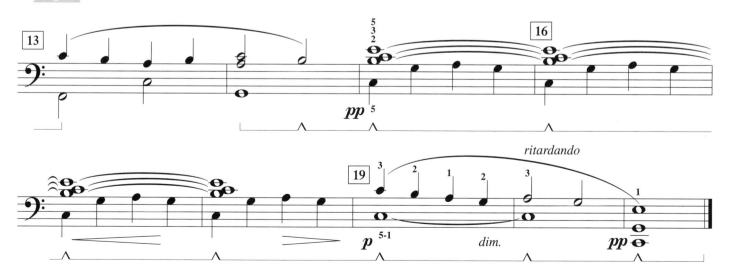

Hello to the Drum

Words by Crystal Bowman
Music by Nancy Faber

Strong march beat

p *growing louder*

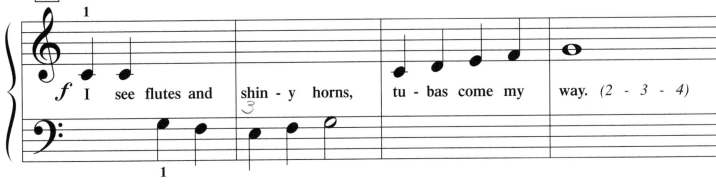

f I see flutes and shin - y horns, tu - bas come my way. *(2 - 3 - 4)*

Teacher Duet: (Student plays 1 octave higher)

FF1602

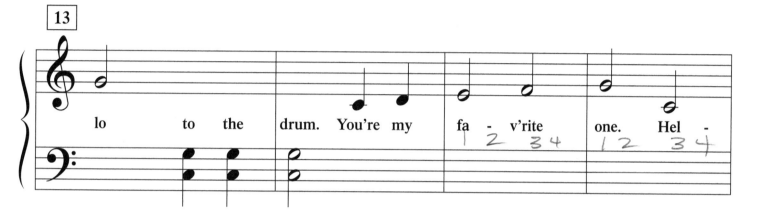

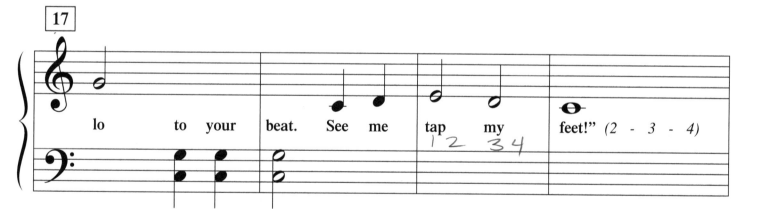

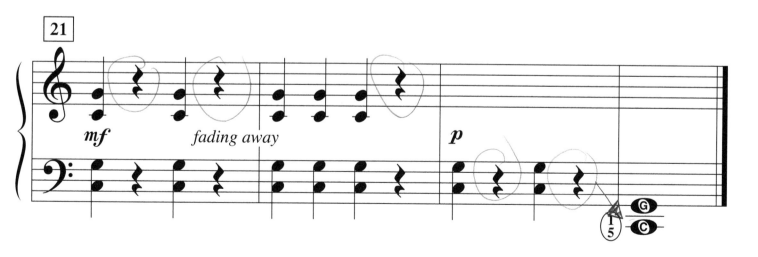

DISCOVERY

Where is the **introduction** and **coda** (special ending) in this piece?

Pony Express

Words and Music
by Nancy Faber

(Move to the
C 5-finger scale.)

(Return L.H. to
Middle C Position.)

FF160

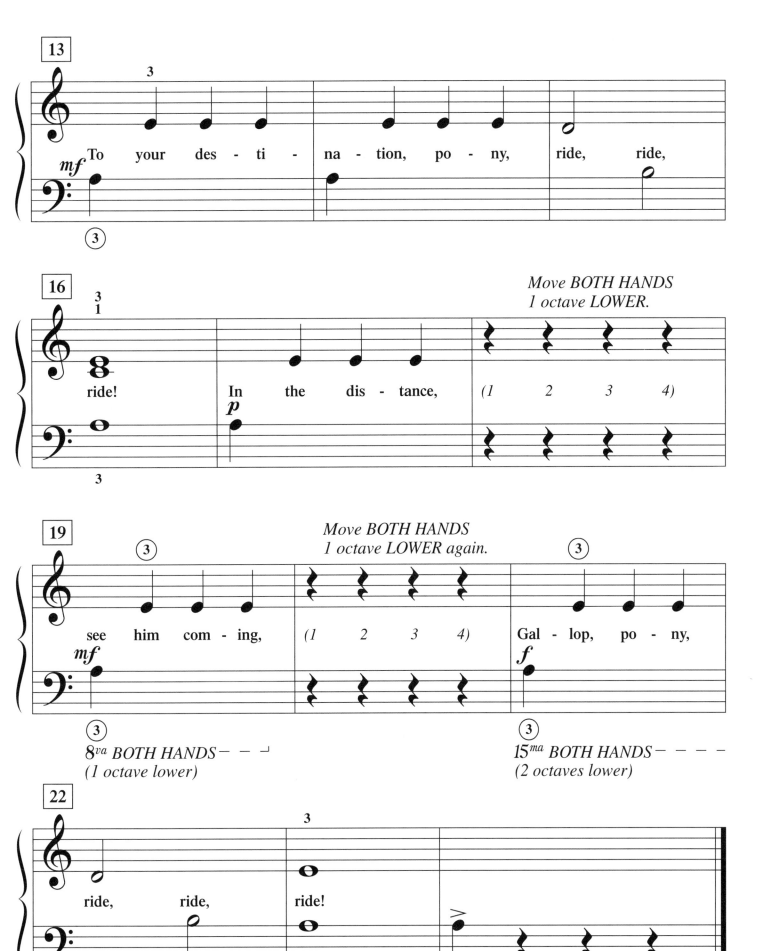

13

To your des - ti - na - tion, po - ny, ride, ride,

mf

16

Move BOTH HANDS
1 octave LOWER.

ride!   In   the   dis - tance,   (1   2   3   4)

p

19

Move BOTH HANDS
1 octave LOWER again.

see   him   com - ing,   (1   2   3   4)   Gal - lop, po - ny,

mf   *f*

8ᵛᵃ BOTH HANDS ‒ ‒ ┘
(1 octave lower)

15ᵐᵃ BOTH HANDS ‒ ‒ ‒ ‒
(2 octaves lower)

22

ride,   ride,   ride!

(15ᵐᵃ) ‒ ‒ ‒ ‒ ‒ ‒ ‒ ‒ ‒ ‒ ‒ ‒ ‒ ‒ ‒ ‒ ┘

 DISCOVERY

Where is there an *accent* in this piece?
Can you brace your L.H. finger 3 with the thumb as you play it?

Cartoon Stories
1. Clown Car

Nancy Faber

Teacher Duet: (Student plays 1 octave higher)

FF160

**Hold the damper pedal
down throughout the piece.**

2. Parakeet Waltz

Slowly gliding

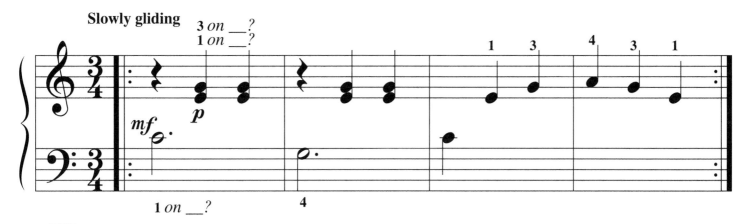

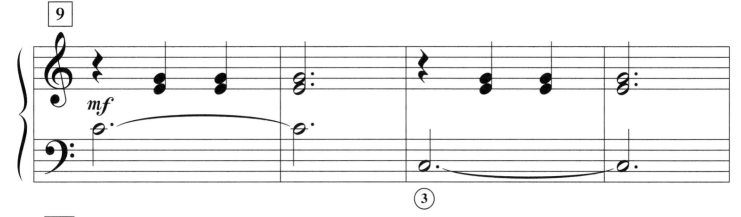

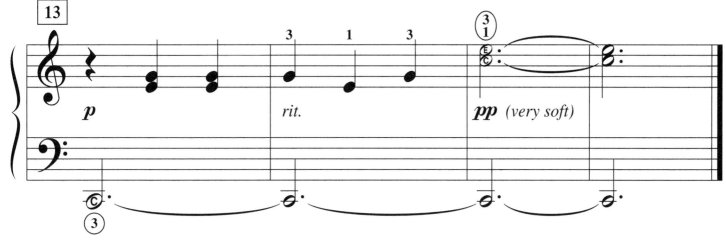

Teacher Duet: (Student plays as written)

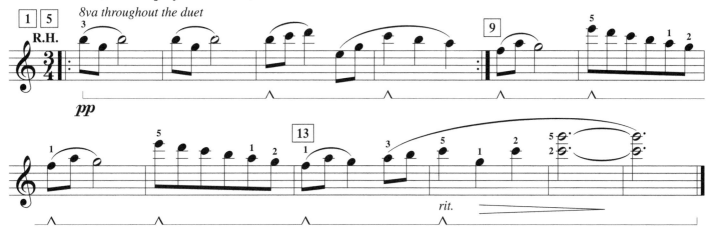

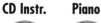

3. Bananappeal

Teacher Duet: (Student plays 1 octave higher)

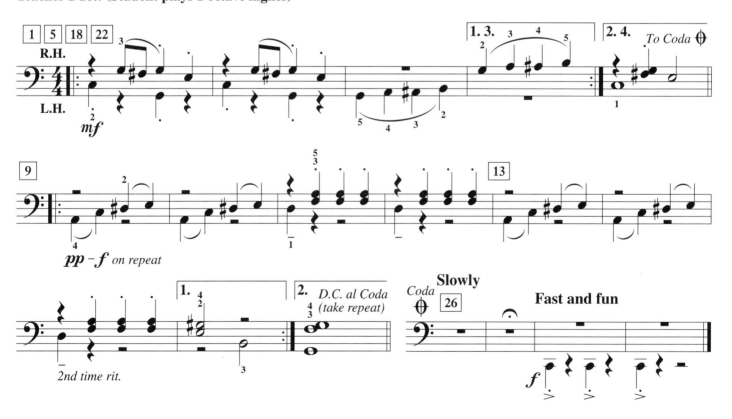

FF1602

Bluebird on My Shoulder
Secondo

U.S. Folk song
Adapted by Nancy Faber

Play as written.

Happily

Lyrics (measures 11–22):

Blue-bird, blue-bird on my shoul-der, blue-bird, blue-bird on my shoul-der,

blue-bird, blue-bird on my shoul-der, sing a song for me. Oh!

"Tweet, tweet, tweet, tweet, tweet, tweet, tweet, tweet," sing a song for me!

FF1602

Bluebird on My Shoulder
Primo

U.S. Folk song
Adapted by Nancy Faber

CD Instr. 23   Piano 24

A Particularly Pleasing Piano Piece

Words by Jennifer MacLean
Music by Nancy Faber

Happily

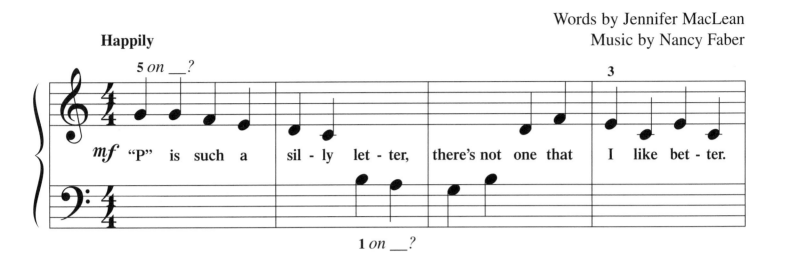

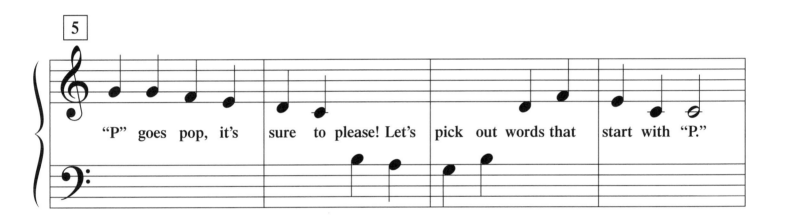

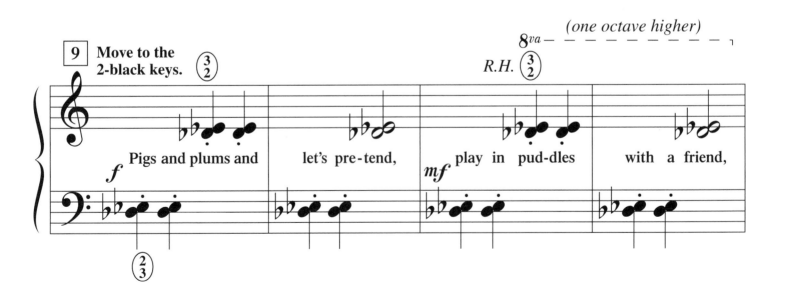

FF1602

Play the highest two-black-key group.

8va ‒ ‒ ‒ ‒ ‒ ‒ ‒ ‒ ‒ ‒ ‒

(two octaves higher)

15ma ‒ ‒ ‒ ‒ ‒ ‒ ‒ ‒ ‒

ritardando

13

R.H.

pur - ple pan - sies in a row, pi - a - nis - si - mo!

p *pp*

17 ⑤ *a tempo*

mf "P" is such a sil - ly let - ter, there's not one that I like bet - ter.

①

21

"P" goes pop, it's sure to please! Let's pick out words that start with "P."

Play the highest
C on the piano!

15ma

ritardando

25

Ping - pong, pen pals, pi - a - nis - si - mo. *Plink!*

p *pp*

G F E D C

① 2 3 4 5

8va ‒ ‒ ‒ ‒ ‒ ‒ ‒ ‒ ‒ ‒ ‒

Play the lowest C 5-finger scale on the piano!

DISCOVERY Point out 3 measures that
have the **quarter rest**.

Squinchy-Pinchy Shoes

Words by Jennifer MacLean
Music by Nancy Faber

FF1602

French Cathedrals

**Hold the damper pedal
down throughout the piece.**

French Folk song
Arranged by Nancy Faber

Joyfully

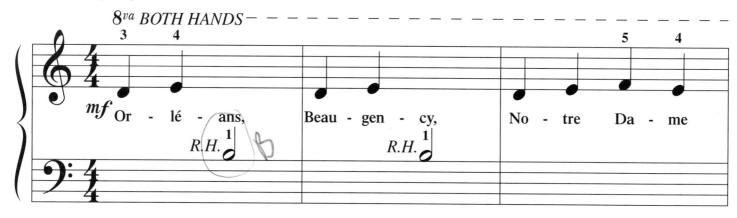

Or - lé - ans,   Beau - gen - cy,   No - tre Da - me

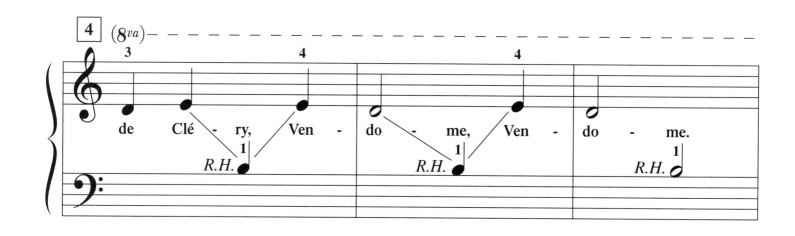

de Clé - ry,   Ven - do - me,   Ven - do - me.

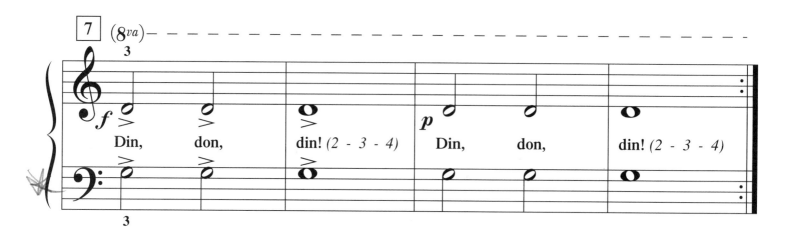

Din,   don,   din! *(2 - 3 - 4)*   Din,   don,   din! *(2 - 3 - 4)*

FF1602

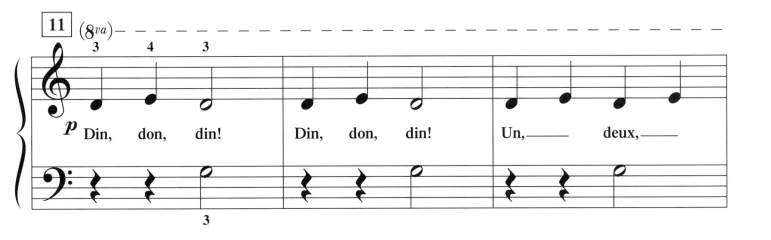

11 *(8va)* —

3   4   3

p Din,   don,   din!   Din,   don,   din!   Un,———   deux,———

3

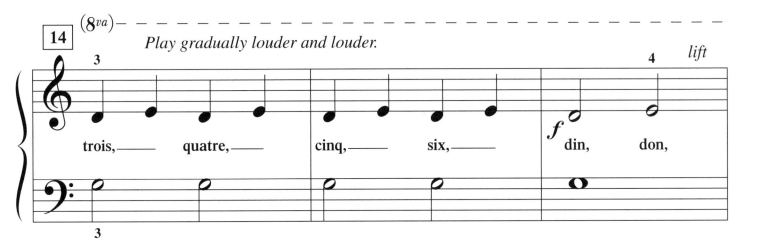

14 *(8va)* —

Play gradually louder and louder.

3   4   *lift*

trois,——   quatre,——   cinq,——   six,——   *f* din,   don,

3

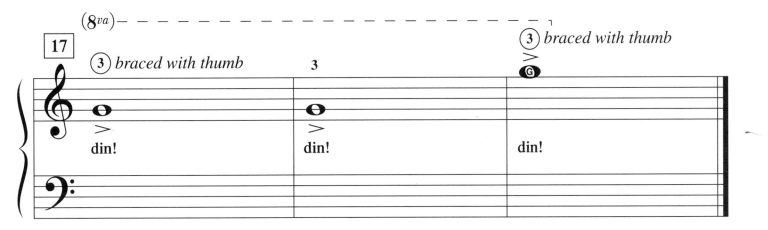

(8va) —

17   ③ *braced with thumb*   ③ *braced with thumb*

③ *braced with thumb*   3   >   G

>   >

din!   din!   din!

DISCOVERY

Where is there an echo in this piece?

Roller Skate Ride

Words by Crystal Bowman
Music by Nancy Faber

Cheerfully

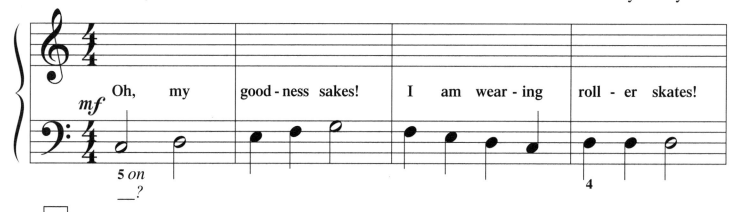

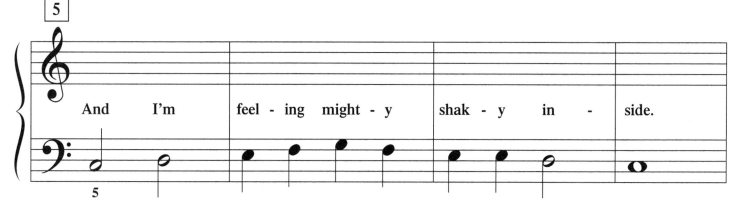

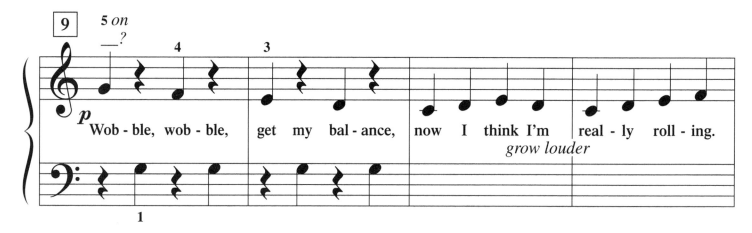

FF160

Where do the *first* two lines of music appear later in the piece?

CD Instr.   Piano

I Love Rain!

**Hold the damper pedal
down throughout the piece.**

Words by Jennifer MacLean
Music by Nancy Faber

Moderately

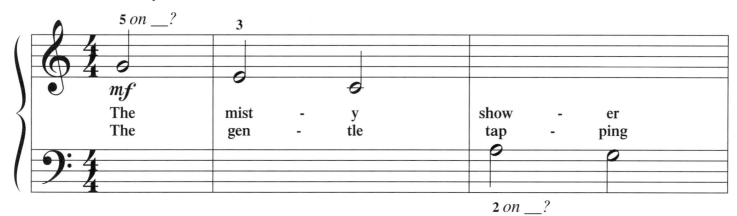

The mist - y show - er
The gen - tle tap - ping

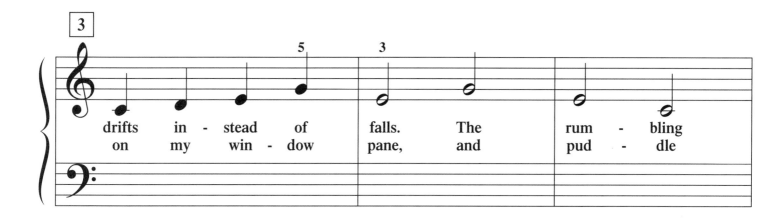

drifts in - stead of falls. The rum - bling
on my win - dow pane, and pud - dle

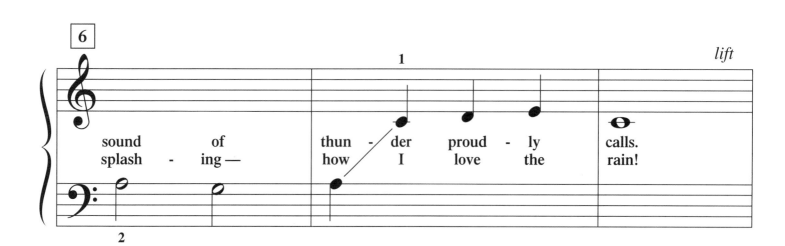

sound of thun - der proud - ly calls.
splash - ing — how I love the rain!

FF160

Note: The teacher may teach this page through demonstration and pattern recognition.

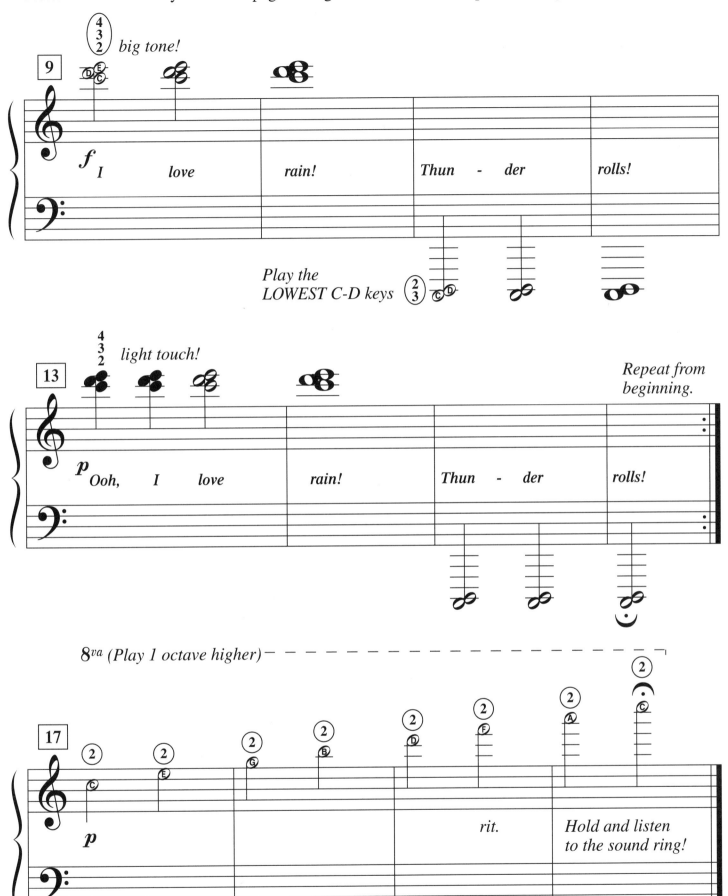

Chugging Choo-Choo

Your teacher will help you find the low L.H. position.
Listen for the great chug-a-lug sounds!

Words and Music
by Nancy Faber

With a great chug-a-lug beat

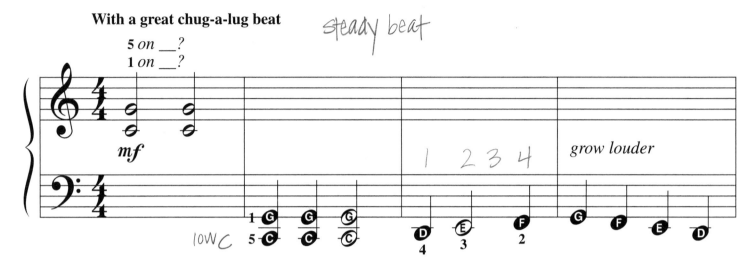

FF160

13 whis - tle is a - blow - in' Hear the chil - dren cry, (2 - 3 - 4)

17 "Whoo - whoo." Choo - choo train, chug chug gin' by. (2 - 3 - 4)

Train whistle position

21 *f* Whoo! *mf* Whoo!

25 *p* Chug - ging choo choo.

as soft as possible

8va - - - - - - -

Play the lowest C on the piano.

DISCOVERY

Point out the following in this piece: *mezzo forte* sign, tie, step, skip, *piano* sign.

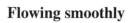

Eternally Music

Words by Jennifer MacLean
Music by Nancy Faber

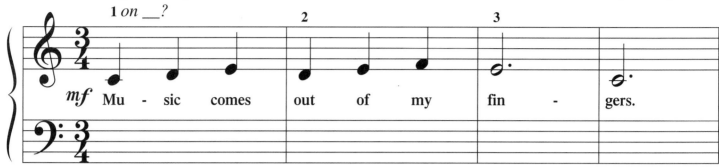

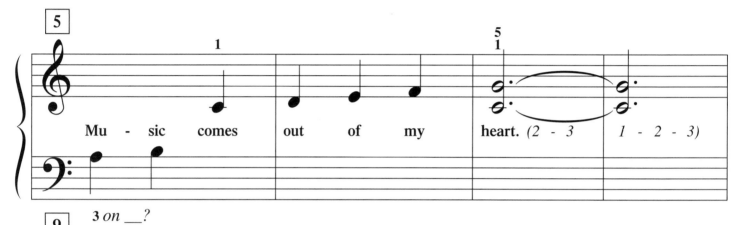

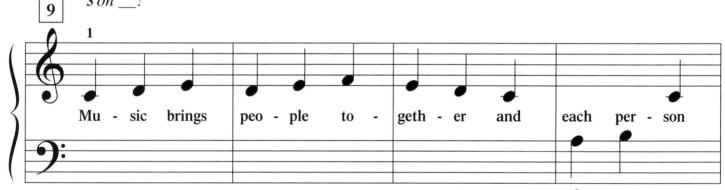

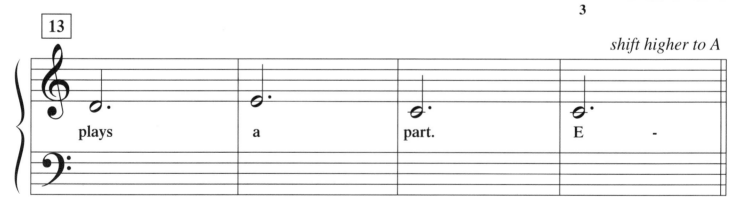

Teacher Duet: (Student plays 1 octave higher)

FF160

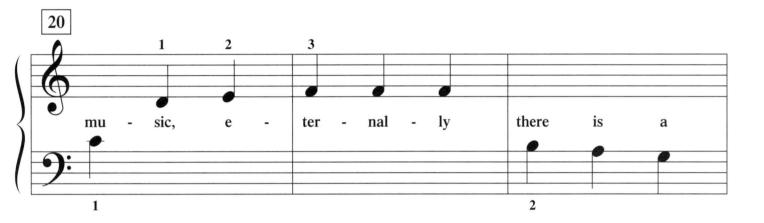

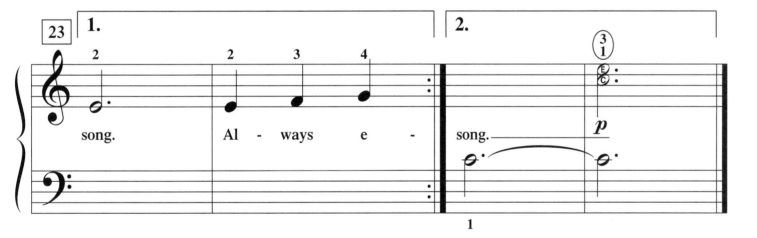

DISCOVERY

Explain the "roadmap" of this piece to your teacher.

Gold Star Dictionary

Circle a gold star when you can pronounce each term and tell your teacher what it means! Have fun listening to the Music Dicitonary Rap on the CD.

1.

accent

Play this note louder.

2.

a tempo

Return to the original tempo (speed).

3.

bass clef

Shows notes below Middle C. Also known as the F clef.

4.

dotted half note

3 beats. Count: 1-2-3.

5.

double bar line

The end of the piece.

6.

fermata

Hold this note longer.

7.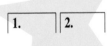

Play the 1st ending with repeat. Then play the 2nd ending, skipping over the 1st.

8.

15ma

Play 2 octaves higher or lower than written.

9.

flat

Play the nearest key to the left. (half step lower)

10. f

forte

f

Loud and strong.

11.

half note

2 beats. Count: 1-2.

12. mf

mezzo forte

mf

Moderately loud.

13.

8va

Play 1 octave higher or lower than written.

FF16

14. $\boldsymbol{p}$ $\boldsymbol{p}$

piano

Softly, gently.

15. *primo*

The higher part in
a 4-hand duet.

16. quarter
note

1 beat. Count: 1.

17. quarter
rest

1 beat of silence.

18. repeat
sign

Play once again.

19. *rit.* *ritardando* *ritard.*

Gradually play slower.

20. *secondo*

The lower part in a
4-hand duet.

21. sharp

Play the nearest key to the right.
(half step higher)

22. tie

A curved line connecting
the same notes. Hold for
the total counts of both.

23. $\frac{4}{4}$ time
signature $\frac{3}{4}$

Top number shows the number of
beats per measure. Lower number
shows the quarter note gets 1 beat.

24. treble
clef

Shows notes above Middle C.
Also known as the G clef.

25. whole
note

4 beats. Count: 1-2-3-4.

GOLD STAR CERTIFICATE

CONGRATULATIONS,
Gold Star Performer!

You have completed the Piano Adventures
Gold Star Performance, Primer Level.

You are now ready to begin
Gold Star Performance, Level 1.

Write your name in the star to celebrate your progress!